MW01503023

THl OFFICER'S GUIDE TO INVESTIGATING ORGANIZED RETAIL THEFT

SEAN GAUGE

CONTENTS

ORGANIZED RETAIL THEFT

INTRODUCTION

When I first started my career as a Police Officer, all rookies at my department were assigned the 'Diablo' beat which included a large shopping mall. The mall was notorious for having retailers that catered to the young urban gangster, a security private security force that was suspect, and the scene of multiple assaults, shootings, and homicides. On a daily basis, often multiple times in the same shift, I would get dispatched to a 'petty theft in-custody, private persons arrest' which meant store security had apprehended a shoplifter. It seemed that every single time I responded the suspect was a 14 year old kid who had put an $8.00 piece of costume jewelry in their purse and left without paying. The loss prevention agent would always insist on prosecuting which resulted in hours of babysitting a juvenile while awaiting a parent or guardian and mountains of paperwork. I hated mall calls. But one day, I responded to a detail that changed my perspective forever. When I arrived for the in-custody, I didn't find a juvenile with two packs of Pokémon cards in their pocket. Instead I was presented with an adult male and an adult female who were still handcuffed, which was rare. Call it intuition, street smarts, experience, or whatever, but even a rookie knows a good crook when you see them and these two had the unmistakable aura attained from multiple police contacts, frequent arrests, and prior incarceration. I learned from the store's loss prevention agents the couple had been apprehended with four different foil lined shopping bags containing hundreds of dollars worth of high end pants. In addition, the male suspect had five different counterfeit driver licenses in his property along with five counterfeit credit cards matching the names on the licenses and the female had three counterfeit driver licenses and credit cards. This was not your typical shoplifting call at the shopping mall. Intrigued, I wanted to investigate more but I hadn't run into this type of thief before-obviously experienced, equipped with sophisticated burglary tools, and in possession of multiple counterfeit documents. I remembered the stories one of my academy instructors used to tell about a Detective from a neighboring jurisdiction known as "The Cat". "The Cat" was famous for taking run of the mill appearing crimes and investigations and turning them into monumental cases involving complex conspiracies and organized criminal networks. One of the stories that had stuck in my mind was that on every shoplifting or petty theft case, "The Cat" would write a search warrant for

2

the suspect's vehicle to look for evidence of other crimes. Well, "The Cat" worked in an affluent city with low calls for service and I worked in a city with a ton of Section 8 housing and more homicides during the summer than his department had in their entire 50 year history. We didn't write search warrants on shoplifting cases. But this case was different. I took the male suspect's key ring, which included a remote from a rental car company, and drove around the parking lots of the mall for 20 minutes with my hand out the window pushing the remote button every couple of seconds until I heard the horn sound. After I found the car, I could see the back of the SUV was full to the ceiling with clothes, electronics, cosmetics, and personal hygiene products. There was no way the sergeant was going to let me write a search warrant on this case but it turned out the male suspect was on probation with a full search clause. I recovered thousands of dollars in merchandise from approximately 15 different identifiable retailers. Even though the shoplifting case turned into something much, much bigger than what I thought it was, I didn't really feel vindicated for taking the time to investigate it until I received a phone call from an organized crime task force telling me that the male suspect was an upper level gang member and that my arrest had led them to a larger counterfeiting ring. I never looked at another 'shoplifting' call the same way again.

THE PROBLEM

Shoplifting. It is often considered a minor crime and, depending on your department and jurisdiction, can draw a lot of resources towards an apparently 'victimless' crime. Sometime the 'victim' is a multi-billion dollar a year retail conglomerate which doesn't attract much sympathy or attention from law enforcement. Many people have shoplifted and it is frequently considered a minor crime. There are a variety of reason people steal from stores. Some of these reasons include youthful indiscretion, crimes of opportunity, and embarrassment. For example, some people would rather risk the consequences of stealing embarrassing items such as condoms, hemorrhoid products, or feminine hygiene products than risk the humiliation of a "price check for personal lubricant on aisle five." Given the current economy, some people steal to survive-trying to provide food for their families or provide them other goods they need. But theft from stores, whether it's called shoplifting or petty theft, is a significant concern to retailers. While multi-billion dollar companies can be less than sympathetic victims, consider the economic cost of 'shrinkage'-loss of goods through theft.

More than $13 billion worth of goods are stolen from retailers each year. That's more than $35 million per day.

There are approximately 27 million shoplifters (or 1 in 11 people) in our nation today. More than 10 million people have been caught shoplifting in the last five years.

Shoplifting affects more than the offender. It overburdens the police and the courts, adds to a store's security expenses, costs consumers more for goods, costs communities lost dollars in sales taxes and hurts children and families.

Shoplifters steal from all types of stores including department stores, specialty shops, supermarkets, drug stores, discounters, music stores, convenience stores and thrift shops.

There is no profile of a typical shoplifter. Men and women shoplift about equally as often.

Approximately 25 percent of shoplifters are kids, 75 percent are adults. 55 percent of adult shoplifters say they started shoplifting in their teens.

Many shoplifters buy and steal merchandise in the same visit. Shoplifters commonly steal from $2 to $200 per incident depending upon the type of store and item(s) chosen.

Shoplifting is often not a premeditated crime. 73 percent of adult and 72 percent of juvenile shoplifters don't plan to steal in advance.

89 percent of kids say they know other kids who shoplift. 66 percent say they hang out with those kids.

Shoplifters say they are caught an average of only once in every 48 times they steal. They are turned over to the police 50 percent of the time.

Approximately 3 percent of shoplifters are "professionals" who steal solely for resale or profit as a business. These include drug addicts who steal to feed their habit, hardened professionals who steal as a life-style and international shoplifting gangs who steal for profit as a business. "Professional" shoplifters are responsible for 10 percent of the total dollar losses.

The vast majority of shoplifters are "non-professionals" who steal, not out of criminal intent, financial need or greed but as a response to social and personal pressures in their life.

The excitement generated from "getting away with it" produces a chemical reaction resulting in what shoplifters describe as an incredible "rush" or "high" feeling. Many shoplifters will tell you that this high is their "true reward," rather than the merchandise itself.

Drug addicts, who have become addicted to shoplifting, describe shoplifting as equally addicting as drugs.

57 percent of adults and 33 percent of juveniles say it is hard for them to stop shoplifting even after getting caught.

Most non-professional shoplifters don't commit other types of crimes. They'll never steal an ashtray from your house and will return to you a $20 bill you may have dropped. Their criminal activity is restricted to shoplifting and therefore, any rehabilitation program should be "offense-specific" for this crime.

Habitual shoplifters steal an average of 1.6 times per week.

Information and statistics provided by the National Association for Shoplifting Prevention (NASP), a non-profit organization; www.shopliftingprevention.org.

ORGANIZED RETAIL THEFT

However, the greatest threat to retailers, whether they are the local mom and pop corner store or the multi-billion dollar chain store, may come from organized retail theft rings. Every year organized groups of professional thieves steal or fraudulently obtain billions of dollars in retail merchandise to resell to consumers. This activity, known as organized retail theft (ORT), is a growing problem for retailers nationwide and the law enforcement entities responsible for investigating and prosecuting these crimes. ORT is an umbrella term which encompasses a variety of crimes including retail theft, fraud, identity theft, gift card fraud, receipt fraud, and bar code switching, among others. These stolen or fraudulently obtained items are resold through a variety of fencing operations such as flea markets, swap meets, pawn shops, and online marketplaces such as eBay and Craigslist. These are not mere shoplifters or petty thieves but professional rings of burglars armed with sophisticated methods of perpetrating billions of dollars of thefts every year. The exact loss from organized retail theft is unknown and difficult to quantify. Some industry and law enforcement estimates include losses of between $15 and $37 billion dollars every year. In addition to the loss of revenue to the retailers, many states and local jurisdictions suffer from the loss of tax revenue associated with stolen items entering the black or gray market economies untaxed. Based on industry statistics and a nominal sales tax rate of 5%, the low end of the range of estimated losses to organized retail theft rings results in a loss of $750,000,000 in tax revenues to states and local jurisdictions. In areas with a higher sales tax, the loss to government is potentially billions of dollars.

The National Retail Federation (NRF) is the world's largest retail association and includes retailers of all sizes, formats and channels of distribution as well as chain restaurants and industry partners from the United States and more than 45 countries abroad. In the United States, the National Retail Federation represents more than 1.6 million American companies which employ nearly 25 million workers. For the last seven years, the NRF has distributed an Organized Retail Crime Survey which garners responses from department and chain stores, as well as, discount, drug, grocery and other specialty retailers. The results of the most recent survey, completed in May 2011 revealed 95% of surveyed retailers reported they had been the victims of organized retails theft in the preceding 12 months, an increase of six percent from the previous year. Perhaps most troubling is that the same survey respondents reported 13% of organized retail crime apprehensions made by retail asset protection employees resulted in violence including physical assault or battery.

The public health risk involved in organized retail theft rings may be substantial. While there are no documented cases of injury or illness from the use of fenced stolen consumer goods, there are instances where sophisticated ORT rings removed or changed expiration dates on items such as baby formula and over the counter medications. The lack of identified cases may be due to the fact the purchaser did not know the goods purchases were stolen and subsequently makes their claim against the manufacturer, or, more likely, no one is willing to report a significant health problem from a product they knowingly or suspected was stolen.

In addition to the economic costs of ORT and the potential health risk to consumers, whether knowing or unknowing, is the connection between the crime and organized crime, gangs, and terrorism. Organized criminal groups, including gangs, are drawn to crimes where the risk of apprehension is offset by the real or potential economic gains. Historically, these groups have involved themselves in a wide assortment of nontraditional criminal enterprises including recycling fraud, identity theft, tobacco smuggling, intellectual property crimes and counterfeiting, and organized retail theft. Where there is an illicit profit to be had, you will inevitably find organized crime willing to commit it. But what if the theft of tooth whitening strips, razor blade cartridges, and baby formula were actually undermining the national security of the United States? As with narcotics, counterfeiting, and other crimes, it is often difficult or impossible to directly tie the proceeds of one specific criminal act to a designated terrorist or a specific attack. However, federal law enforcement agencies have expressed increasing concern over the disposition of funds from crimes such as organized retail theft, once they reach specific target countries or regions which are known to harbor or assist terrorist activities. For example, an investigation into the Jamal Trading Company in Phoenix AZ revealed a money laundering operation which transferred funds from an ORT ring into Iraq, Jordan, and Lebanon-all areas of insurgent or terrorist activity. The ringleader of the organization and 15 co-conspirators had profited from the sale of stolen infant formula with a retail value in excess of $22 million dollars. In another case an organized retail theft ring involving suspect Mohammed Khalil Ghalil revealed the profits from stolen infant formula and other high value items were smuggled out of the United States to financial institutions in Jordan, Egypt,

13

and Palestine. The Department of Homeland Security alleged several members of the organization were directly ties to terrorist acts and organizations. In another example, the FBI's Joint Terrorism Task Force (JTTF) investigated a case where a group known as the Hamed Organization was directly involved in the fencing of stolen and contraband goods such as infant formula, computers, Global Positioning System (GPS) devices and cigarettes and then funneling the proceeds to the Palestinian territories. While it is extremely difficult to trace and prove the crime of material support to terrorism, it is believed that some of these cases demonstrated the material support of terrorist groups through organized retail theft.

TOP 10 CITIES FOR ORGANIZED RETAIL CRIME

According to the National Retail Federation the top cities for organized retail theft, in alphabetical order, include:

Atlanta, GA

Chicago, IL

Dallas, TX

Houston, TX

Las Vegas, NV

Los Angeles, CA

Miami/Ft. Lauderdale, FL

New York, NY/Northern NJ

Philadelphia, PA

Phoenix, AZ

Las Vegas and Phoenix are two new additions to the list, replacing San Francisco and the Baltimore-DC-Northern Virginia corridor, which both continue to be areas with high organized retail crime activity.

Compounding the problem of organized retail theft is the lack of a common definition. What exactly is it and who defines it? More importantly, who investigates and enforces these crimes, which reportedly cost the country billions of dollars?

Organized retail theft is commonly used in the retail industry and among state and local law enforcement agencies to encompass those crimes which affect the consumer. Some ORT definitions broadly include shoplifting, organized criminal rings, gift card fraud, fraudulent returns, and cargo theft, among others. While there is no agreed upon definition of ORT, this manual focuses on the investigation and enforcement of crimes associated with the federal definition, specifically:

(1) the violation of a state law or prohibition on retail merchandise theft or shoplifting, if the violation consists of the theft of quantities of items that would not normally be purchased for personal use or consumption and for the purpose of reselling the items or for reentering the items into commerce;

(2) the receipt, possession, concealment, bartering, sale, transport, or disposal of any property that is known or should be known to have been taken in violation of paragraph (1); or

(3) the coordination, organization, or recruitment of persons to undertake the conduct described in paragraph (1) or (2).

ORT is distinguished from shoplifting in that amateur shoplifter tend to steal merchandise for personal use or consumption. Criminals involved in ORT are professional thieves who profit by staling merchandise and reselling through legitimate, semi-legitimate, or illegal means for the sole purpose of profit.

Working an organized retail theft case can be frustrating. There is frequently a lack of understanding of the greater issue by law enforcement leadership, especially when faced with diminishing resources and other more visible types of crimes. Some in the law enforcement community feel that because retailers have their own asset protection bureau that they should maintain responsibility for prevention and apprehension efforts. But if the crime of organized retail theft were narcotics or stolen vehicles or residential burglary rings, the emphasis on investigation and enforcement would be substantially greater than it is with ORT.   Most law enforcement leadership would not tolerate the presence of these organized crime groups in their jurisdictions and would allocate resources appropriately to address them. However, when it comes to ORT, many law enforcement agencies continue to view the problem as a simply a property crimes, petty theft, or simply shoplifting. Faced withed a lack of leadership, it is relatively easy for some law enforcement agencies to "wash their hands" of these crimes and move on to the current high visibility threat in their jurisdiction. However, failing to address the issue can raise other long term consequences including:

Failing to address an entry level crime from which juveniles and first time offenders may graduate into more serious criminal acts

Retail theft may indirectly fuel the local narcotics trade because it provides the income some drug users use to acquire their drugs

Retailers in economically disadvantages neighborhoods can suffer substantial losses from theft, seriously impacting their operating margins and forcing closure, resulting in a loss of tax revenue to the city and resulting unemployment

Permissive attitudes and policies towards retail theft can cause an increase in those types of crimes subsequently consuming a disproportionate among of scant resources in processing offenders apprehended by store security and loss prevention agents

Organized retail crimes rings do no limit themselves to preying upon retailers and may commit additional crimes including fraud, identity theft, vehicle theft, and counterfeiting in order to abet their primary mission

Small scale appearing thefts may in fact be part of a larger organized criminal conspiracy including traditional organized crime, gangs, and international terrorism

Organized retail theft investigations invariably involve the participation of merchant representatives such as loss prevention or security departments from private companies. This commonly is an uncomfortable position for many law enforcement agencies to be in-working with civilians to assist in the investigation of complex criminal organizations. However, both the investigating law enforcement agencies and the commercial entity's priorities are in alignment when it comes to these cases. The law enforcement agency has a mandate to investigate and enforce applicable laws against a sophisticated criminal threat in their jurisdiction and the retailer has a vested interest in maintaining the viability as a business.

Another factor which commonly clouds the waters in ORT investigations is the lack of clear delineation among federal law enforcement agencies when it comes to investigative responsibility. The Federal Bureau of Investigation (FBI) has, among its many other responsibilities, the power to investigate the federal crime of interstate transportation of stolen property. However, Immigrations and Customs Enforcement (ICE) has enforcement responsibilities for the accompanying crimes of money laundering and exporting of the same stolen merchandise. While some multijurisdictional task forces have had success involving both agencies, there is no designated lead federal agency with primary responsibility for investigating organized retail theft. Neither the FBI or ICE have dedicated organized retail theft resources, however both have implemented efforts to increase the tracking of these types of crimes in their respective case management systems.

State and local law enforcement bear the primary responsibility for investigating and prosecuting organized retail crime. However, as the scope of the crime has increased, so has the involvement of federal law enforcement agencies. As retail criminals are no longer selling goods simply out of the trunks of their cars or at local flea markets but are using interstate transportation routes to move stolen goods, so increases the federal interest in these types of investigations.

The challenge that presents to law enforcement is not the kid stealing a pack of gum, but organized criminal enterprises which imperil the retailer, the consumer, and the community. Sophisticated rings of criminals deliberately target certain merchants and their high value products for theft, depriving the retailer of revenue, exposing the consumer to potentially expired or adultered materials, and reducing the tax revenues of jurisdictions across the United States. The criminal groups are the basis of organized retail theft. But this crime is much more complex than it initially appears and is plagued by a number of factors including cross-jurisdictional issues, a lack of available resources to properly investigate, competing priorities with other traditional crimes, and a misunderstanding of the problem by state and local law enforcement agencies.

CASE EXAMPLE: ROSEMONT WHOLESALE

Hayward, CA-In 2007 federal agents from Immigrations and Customs enforcement executed a search warrant at Rosemont Wholesale. Inside the business' warehouse investigators discovered more than $9 million dollars in stolen merchandise including baby formula, over the counter medications such as Tylenol, razor blades, and teeth whitening products. The volume of stolen merchandise was such that it took 12 tractor trailer loads to haul it all away. The recovered merchandise hadn't been taken by a cargo theft ring but instead had been stolen by professional shoplifters and drug addicts seeking to fuel their addiction.

This case was not discovered by ICE or any other federal law enforcement agency. It was investigated by the loss prevention departments of several major retailers including Safeway, Target, and Wal-Mart. Recognizing they were being victimized by an organized group of criminal, these retail investigators decided to focus on attacking the source of the problem, the fencing operation, instead of on traditional apprehension of the lower level thieves. Employing law enforcement techniques, loss prevention agents from the involved stores allowed shoplifters to leave their stores with the stolen merchandise and surveilled them to several retail stores in Oakland, CA. They observed suspects entering carrying boxes and bags of merchandise but leaving empty handed. They were eventually able to surveil the shop owners to the warehouse in Hayward, CA where they established long term surveillance from a clandestine location. In the middle of the night, loss prevention agents would rifle through the trash bins of the warehouse locating thousands of discarded security stickers and label.

When federal law enforcement agencies eventually raided the business they discovered a sophisticated cleaning operation with multiple people engaged full-time in removing identifying labels and stickers from the stolen merchandise. Once cleaned, the items were repackaged and sold as wholesale good to accomplices and unsuspecting vendors across the United States.

Rosemont Wholesale had been in business nearly ten years before the organization was dismantled. The owner, Hassan Swaid, was sentenced to 78 years in prison. Ironically, Swaid's sentencing was largely due to his violations of money laundering statutes for structuring cash deposits under the $10,000 reporting threshold, filing false tax returns, and tax evasion.

THE GOODS

ORT groups target many different products such as infant formula, over-the-counter pharmaceuticals, such as pain relievers; cigarettes; disposable razor blades; teeth-whitening strips; diabetic test strips; DVDs; and Nicorette/Nicoderm chewing gum. All of these products are small, easy to conceal, and worth large amounts of money when sold through fencing operations. The acronym CRAVED is commonly used to identify the desirable attributes of targeted items.

C-Concealable. While some ORT rings practice 'grab and run' tactics, many still use the tried and true methods of concealing multiple high value items on their persons or in specially designed containers.

R-Removable. In order for the thief the steal the item, it must be capable of being easily removed. Retailers have gone to great lengths to attempt to impair the ability of frequently stolen items from being easily removed but increasing the bulk of items or locking them in cases.

A-Available. There must be an available quantity of the item.

V-Valuable. In order to be targeted by a professional thief the item must have sufficient value to justify the risk of apprehension.

E-Enjoyable. Enjoyment is a relative term but usually speaks to the demand for a particular item and the subjective perception of its value. A fifteen year old male would likely have greater enjoyment from the latest video game release than a 70 year old woman.

D-Disposable. The professional thief must have an existing method of converting the stolen property into cash or the perception that the item is easily convertible.

Professional thieves include price point information into their decisions about what they are going to steal. Items which are in high demand tend to command near retail prices in the secondary market.

CONSUMABLES

Alcohol and Tobacco (both for personal use and for re-sale)

Energy drinks (Red Bull)

BEAUTY AND HYGIENE SUPPLIES

Aveeno lotion

Cover Girl cosmetics

Crest Whitestrips

deodorants

Oil of Olay

Oral B replacement heads

perfumes

EPT pregnancy test kits

Pureology hair products

RoC skin care products

CONSUMER ELECTRONICS

Apple notebooks, iPads, and iPods,

batteries (AA, AAA, and lithium)

Blu-ray players and movies

Braun electric razors

cell phones

computer accessories

digital cameras

DVD/Bluray players

GPS units

Kitchen Aid mixers

laptop computers

music CDs

printer ink cartridges

video game consoles and games

vacuum cleaners (particularly high end models like Dyson))

CLOTHING/ACCESSORIES

denim jeans

North Face jackets

Victoria's Secret lingerie

handbags

high end shoes

sunglasses

OVER-THE-COUNTER (OTC) MEDICATIONS, SUPPLEMENTS, AND TEST KITS

Abreva

Advil

Aleve

Alli weight-loss pills

Benadryl

Claritin

diabetic test strips

dietary weight gain products for muscle building

dietary weight loss products

Immodium

Lotrimin

Pepcid AC

Prilosec

Primatene

Rogaine

smoking cessation products (Nicorette)

Sudafed (both for resale and for methamphetamine production)

Tylenol

Visine

Zantac

OTHER GOODS

candles

chain saws (particularly Husqvarna)

Power tools (DeWalt 18V batteries and 6-tool Combo Kit, electric welders)

golf balls

art supplies

veterinary products such as flea medications

toner cartridges

THE THIEF

CASUAL CRIMINAL

The public perception of someone who steals from a retail establishment is the common shoplifter who steals out of need or poor impulse control. Some believe that stealing is 'not a big deal' and that shoplifting is a different, lesser crime than theft. In fact, the very term shoplifter may actually perpetuate societies, and law enforcement leaderships, misunderstanding of the problem.

PROFESSIONAL BOOSTER RINGS

The professional thief, commonly referred to as a 'booster' is the heart of the problem. According to the asset protections departments of some major retailers, ORT rings have targeted multiple stores in a single day and chose to target shopping malls and large retail complexes due to the number of merchants located there. Some booster rings are able to victimize between 8 and 15 retailers in a single day. They represent the greatest likelihood of contact with law enforcement as a result of apprehension. Investigating boosters and booster rings presents the greatest opportunity for law enforcement intervention and investigation.

According to information obtained from US Immigrations and Customs enforcement investigators following the interview and debrief of a number of boosters, and asset protection agents from a number of large retailers, two generally recognized levels of professional shoplifter/booster rings have been identified:

Lower Level: A lower level booster is not a common shoplifter and is not stealing for the excitement. They are professional thieves who work in smaller groups, sometimes with only one or two accomplices. Boosters at this level are frequently addicted to drugs and will only steal enough products to pay for their daily fix. Low level boosters will commonly sell their stolen goods to a street fence for 20-30% of the retail value. Even though they are considered to be at the bottom rung of professional thieves, low level boosters can steal between $100-2,000 per day which generates $20-600 in cash for the thief.

Upper Level: The upper level booster ring may include up to 25 or more professional shoplifters, however it is much more common to find the group comprised of between four to six males and females. These groups are often recruited, trained, supervised, and directed by a street or mid-level fence. The group operates at the direction of the fence who will instruct the booster ring towards specific stores and particular merchandise. The group may have a 'fence sheet' or 'shopping list' of desirable items they are looking for including razor blades, diabetic test strips, infant formula, teeth whitening products, cosmetics, and over-the-counter medications. An experienced male is usually the team leader and is responsible for handling the logistics of the group including transportation, food, and lodging. The group travels to a target city or area, secures lodging, usually in a hotel, and spends the next four to ten days stealing from stores in the area. Hotels of choice tend to be major motel chains with easy freeway access and parking adjacent to their rooms for easy and covert loading and unloading of merchandise. Rental vehicles are frequently used to travel to the target city and passenger van, large SUVs, and full size cars are preferred due to their storage capacity. Some groups specifically schedule their visits to arrive on a Thursday and leave on a Monday in order to take advantage of larger weekend crowds at retail locations and shopping malls. The boosters may employ 'booster boxes', customized bags or containers modified with metal foil to circumvent in-store security measures. The group may also use other tactics such as placing higher value items inside other lower value containers known as 'box stuffing', return stolen merchandise for credit or gift cards commonly referred to as return fraud, and placing fake bar code stickers for lower priced goods over the legitimate bar code which is known as ticket switching. One or more members of the group may act as lookouts or try to distract store employees which the others remove merchandise. The goods may actually be collected by the group members and then actually removed from the store by another member or members known as the 'mule.' The merchandise may actually be moved from 'mule' to 'mule' several times before it actually leaves the store. At the conclusion of a day's worth of heists, the stolen goods are temporarily house in a self-storage unit rented by the team leader. At the end of the operation the stolen goods are removed from the storage unit and loaded into rental trucks for return to their home city and subsequent disposition with the established fencing operation. The boosters can expect to receive 10% to 25% of the value of the stolen goods for their efforts. The fence is responsible for having the stolen merchandise 'cleaned' which involves removing retail price tags, electronic article surveillance (EAS) tags, stickers, and any other merchant identification tags, devices, or symbols. The 'cleaners' used acetone, commonly known as finger nail polish remover, and razor blades to remove any sign the merchandise was stolen from a retailer. In some instances expiration dates are changed and/or counterfeit bar code labels are applied to extend the shelf-life of the stolen goods. Depending on the fence's connections for re-introducing stolen items into the marketplace the fence may divide the 'cleaned' items into two categories. Items which are expired or have a rapidly approaching expiration date and items which were damaged will be sold to lower level fencing operations such as discounters, liquidators, and flea market vendors. Items which are intact are consolidated and may be sold to upper level fences.

FRAUD SCHEMES

An emerging trend with sophisticated ORT booster rings is changing the universal price code (UPC) barcode stickers on merchandise so it rings up differently at checkout. Thieves use commercially available barcode generator software and printers to create fake barcodes and place them over the legitimate code. The practice is commonly called ticket switching and is difficult to detect unless the retailer actually touches the product and detects the fake sticker and recognizes the price is much lower than it should be. Other associated methods include the use of stolen or counterfeit credit cards and identification documents to obtain merchandise. These criminals usually work for buyers, fences, or ring leaders who have lists of specific products in mind that are not easily stolen such as high end vacuum cleaners and power tools.

Return fraud is another common method of profiting from stolen merchandise. Many retailers do not require a receipt for the return of merchandise. A booster ring can steal items from one branch of a store, drive to another branch in a neighboring city, and return the merchandise. While many retailers will not issue cash for merchandise returned with a receipt, they will issue a store gift card for the amount of the returned merchandise. A simple search on the internet marketplace craigslist.org reveals there are multiple outlets for gift card buyers who offer to pay up to 70% of the face value of the gift card.

Return fraud can also be accomplished through the use of counterfeit receipts. A Google search for "fake receipt" reveals a number of different websites which offer a range of services from fake receipt templates to the actual manufacture and shipment of counterfeit receipts. Depending on the store's policy, a booster may receive cash or gift cards for items returned with a receipt.

Return fraud allow booster rings to bypass the traditional fencing operation and net the criminals a much higher return than they would normally receive. Information from retail security organizations and federal law enforcement sources indicate a booster expects to receive 10% to 25% of the retail value. By using return fraud, a criminal can expect to receive 70% to 100% of the retail value of the stolen goods. However, these methods entail an increased chance of apprehension as the thief is required to stay in the store longer and there is greater risk of detection from well trained retail staff and loss prevention departments.

INSIDERS

Sometimes, boosters may conspire with current or former store employees who assist the ring with their crimes. This assistance may come in the form of committing outright theft themselves or facilitating the booster rings thefts by leaving doors unlocked, providing alarm codes, and/or duplicating keys. A colluding employee may also provide boosters with information which could assist them including new product arrival, management schedules, and the days and times loss prevention agents are deployed inside the store.

The direct proportion of retail 'shrinkage' due to direct employee theft and/or collusion is not known. However, a 2010 National Retail Security survey reported that responding retailers estimated approximately 45% of retail losses were due to employee theft. Furthermore, the survey results indicated that the respondents reports more than 18% of internal losses involved employees assisting people outside of the retail location. It is unknown what percentage of that 18% of involved collusion with organized retail theft rings.

METHODS

The internet blog rorta.net, under the subheading nonnormative economics, gives a detailed list of specific methods and techniques of stealing from stores. While many of the techniques are outdated or seem farfetched, the website dedicates an entire section on the ins and outs of both amateur and professional shoplifting. The articles even feature postings from self described loss prevention agents from major retailers who give specific instructions on how to circumvent the security features and policies of their store. The methods listed in the rorta.net blog can be broken down in several major subtypes:

"ACCIDENTAL" STEALING

In "Accidental" stealing, a thief takes his place in the queue with the items he intends to steal, and pays for only one of those items while holding what he intends to steal in full view to cause confusion (or places said items into his pockets), while avoiding suspicion due to his apparent intention of payment. In the unlikely event of being caught, the thief can simply pass off the attempt at stealing as accidental. This method is also referred to as "left handing," a reference to the stolen item being held in the left hand while payment is made with the right.

GRAB AND RUN

A common shoplifting technique is known by the loss prevention community as a "grab and run." Simply put, a shoplifter enters a retail establishment usually with prior knowledge of what he is looking for. The shoplifter moves very quickly toward the merchandise he or she wishes to steal. Once the shoplifter has found the merchandise, he or she proceeds toward the nearest store exit, usually while running. Due to the short amount of time that the shoplifter is inside the store, persons who attempt this scam are seldom caught or, in some cases, even detected. Less common is for a group of people to rush into a store, grab as much merchandise as possible, and then rush out, sometimes referred to as a 'flash rob' after the thankfully short lived 'flash mob' phenomenon. The speed at which this happens as well as the large number of people involved makes this approach difficult to stop.

CONCEALMENTS/BOX STUFFING

BABY STROLLER BOXES

This scam involves the use of baby stroller boxes, which tend to be quite large in size. A would-be shoplifter removes the stroller from the box and proceeds to conceal a large amount of merchandise inside. The would-be shoplifter then reseals the box and takes it to a checkout aisle, where he pays the purchase price for the stroller. If the scam is successful the would-be shoplifter walks out of the retailer with concealed merchandise still inside the stroller box.

BAGGING, SIMPLE

The '"Simple Bagging"' Tactic is when a would-be shoplifter bags the item in a bag that they have brought into the store (ex. purse or shopping bag from another store). This generally is done while no one is watching.

FITTING ROOM BAGGING

Typically this scam is seen in large clothing retailers. This scam generally preys upon the common Loss Prevention policy of prohibiting the apprehension of shoplifters when concealment is not actually seen by an investigator. The shoplifter enters a retail establishment with a large bag, and then selects a large amount of merchandise and takes it to a fitting room. Once inside, the shoplifter conceals the merchandise into the bag out of sight of store employees and store investigators.

This technique is very effective due to the fact that most department stores do not supervise the dressing room (they do not check the amount of clothes a person has before and after using a dressing room). Also, because it is common to leave clothes in the dressing room that one does not wish to purchase, entering a dressing room with clothing and exiting with none will arouse no suspicion.

USE OF TOOLS AND MECHANICAL ADJUNCTS

BARCODE COUNTERFEITING

To commit barcode counterfeiting the shoplifter will bring in pre-made barcodes from low value items. They are then applied over the barcodes on higher value items. This allows the shoplifter to go through the check out process, make a payment, have any security tags deactivated by the clerk and walk out without any suspicious behavior. The shoplifter might be working with the checkout clerk to ensure the incorrect prices are not noticed.

BARCODE SWITCHING

This is when a shoplifter switches the tags/barcodes between two pieces of merchandise most likely putting the cheaper tag on the product they wish to obtain

BOOSTER BOXES (BAG)

A booster box is a device that allows a would-be shoplifter to conceal a large quantity of merchandise on his person. These boxes are lined with metal or some other substance to prevent security tags from setting off the security gates at the exit.

GIFT CARD CLONING

In this scam, a normal store gift card with no value attached is stolen from a store. The shoplifter then clones the magnetic strip on the back of the gift card and makes a copy or copies of it. The original gift card is then returned to the store by the shoplifter. The gift card is activated once purchased by another customer, and the dollar amount applied to the legitimate gift card is passed to all the cloned gift cards.

RAZOR FINGER

This technique involves using a razor blade to remove or destroy security tags on merchandise. The razor blade is taped onto the fingers with medical tape to give the appearance of an injury. The blade is then used to cut off or destroy the security tags.

SCAMS

COUPON RETURNS

One of the more common scams involves returning items that were paid for partially with coupons. Some stores, including Target, refund the entire item amount, including the amount discounted by coupons. Shoplifters involved in this scam often shop at multiple stores, and have family members return items so that no suspicion is aroused.

DEFECTIVE SOFTWARE SCAM

A person buys a piece of software from a computer store, exits, opens software, and records serial number/CD key for single license of the software purchased. After at least a few hours the same person re-enters the store he bought the software at and complains to customer service that the installation disc is defective. Most computer store policies allow same-item exchange for opened computer software, so person is given a different copy of the same software. The scammer now has two licenses after only paying for one. A more convincing variation includes intentionally nicking the top layer of installation CD/DVD, rendering the discs actually defective before exchanging it.

FAKE RETURN

Sometimes shoplifters will actually gather an item from the selling floor and try to receive money for it without a receipt at the return station. Although this method is not as fool proof as the receipt matching method, it is very effective particularly when done to an inexperienced cashier. Usually the shoplifter will start complaining to the cashier about his inability to return the merchandise. Typically the shoplifter will state that he lost his receipt or threaten the cashier by stating that he wants to talk to the employee's supervisor. To avoid confrontation the cashier will ring up the return and give the shoplifter the value of the merchandise.

RECEIPT MATCHING

The receipt matching scam involves using receipts to match merchandise codes from the receipt to items found in a store. Most retailers use company specific merchandise codes on their merchandise so store personnel can identify the location more quickly and efficiently. Additionally the merchandise is used to verify merchandise that was purchased at a particular retailer during a return. This information is printed onto the receipts of purchased merchandise. Typically shoplifters will search either retailer's parking lot or trashcans looking for receipts that have a high dollar item on it. The shoplifter then enters the store and compares the code on the receipt to the codes printed on the merchandise in the store. Once the shoplifter finds a match he will take the merchandise to the return area and receive money for it.

THE TOOLS

Recognition of the tools used by boosters and ORT rings can help identify the professional thief and differentiate them from someone who steals simply because of greed or opportunity. The possession and/or use of these tools are also a key differentiator when charging and prosecuting an apprehended suspect. For example, in California, the use or possession of tools can elevate the misdemeanor crime of petty theft to the felony crime of burglary.

Many methods used by organized retail theft rings do not require the use of sophisticated tools or techniques. Some techniques simply rely on concealment or speed to carry out their thefts. However, as retailers attempt to protect their merchandise they are turning to technology in an effort to thwart the thieves. Many retailers use inventory control devices such as electronic article surveillance (EAS) and radio frequency identification (RFID.)

EAS- Are tags or stickers that are applied by retailers to merchandise. These tags are removed or deactivated by the retailer's employees when the item is purchased. At the exits of the store, a detection system sounds an alarm or otherwise alerts the staff when it senses tags which have not been properly deactivated. EAS tags come in many different shapes and sizes designed to meet the needs of the retailers and can involve the use of magnetic materials, radio frequency, and microwave signals.

In order to reduce the burden and cost associated with retailers installing the EAS tags themselves, many manufacturers and distributors of commonly stolen items are applying the tags during the packaging of the goods and prior to delivery to the merchant. This process is referred to as source tagging and has several benefits, not the least of which is the integration of the security devices into the product packaging making it more difficult for the booster to detect and/or remove prior to stealing it.

RFID-These devices are small for the devices most frequently used to automatically identify and track merchandise. Many large retailers, such as Wal-Mart, use them to manage their supply chains. The RFID tag is comprised of two parts; one for storing and processing information and an antenna for sending and receiving signals. Some RFID devices do not require an external power source and are powered by the scanners used to read them. In addition to being able to determine the source of stolen goods by reading the information from the RFID tags, some retailers have integrated the tags into their loss prevention efforts. Using a combination of surveillance cameras and sophisticated behavior and pattern recognition software RFID tags can assist in apprehension of boosters.

In order to counteract the effectiveness of these anti-theft devices, boosters have turned to technology themselves to overcome the risk of detection. Some boosters and ORT rings use booster bags or boxes to facilitate their crime. Booster bags and boxes originated as containers with hidden traps or compartments which allowed merchandise to be quickly concealed inside while retaining an outward appearance that the container was intact. For example, some very early booster boxes were wrapped as Christmas presents with a hidden flap in the bottom where product could be placed. However, in modern times someone walking into a store with a gift wrapped package is likely to immediately alert loss prevention agents. So boosters have developed modern equivalents to the old booster box which allows for concealment of stolen merchandise and a way to defeat the merchants' electronic sensors. These new and improved booster bags are commonly modified to give the outward appearance of belonging to the targeted, or a nearby, store. Store employees may be less likely to stop and question boosters carrying shopping bags from the store, or an adjacent retailer, because they assume that the merchandise has indeed been paid for. The bags are frequently lined with metal foil and duct tape which can cause interference between the anti-theft tags and the sensors located near the exit. Sophisticated ORT rings may also use other radio frequency interfering materials such as metal mesh Faraday bags or fabric. Faraday bags, meshes, and fabrics are constructed of metal fibers with electromagnetic field impeding capabilities. They are commonly used by law enforcement to preserve and examine mobile phones in a forensic environment. These same materials can also be used by boosters. ORT rings have also modified the original booster box or bag and incorporated the same shielding materials into brief cases, computer bags, purses, and backpacks.

Boosters may also use a number of commercially available or improvised tools to remove theft sensors and to extract small high value items from their bulky packaging. Knives, razor blades, scissors, and other cutting implements are common tools used not only to assist in the theft, but can also be used to deter loss prevention agents during apprehension. Detailed instructions for the creation and use of improvised tools can be found on YouTube. Boosters can also use other tools to remove the anti-theft sensors. These are the same tools used by the retailers to remove the anti-theft tags at the point of sale and can be purchased from a number of sources located during a simple internet search.

Other fraud related crimes can be more equipment intensive. UPC counterfeiting and receipt fraud require a computer, printer, and specialized papers in order to manufacture the false documentation. These items may be found in temporary storage locations used by the ORT group such as hotel and motel rooms and self service storage facilities. Similarly, gift card fraud may entail the use of a computer and card reader to identify or alter the unique number associated with the card. The requirement to use these sophisticated technological means also presents an opportunity for law enforcement to

seek search warrants for identified locations in order to search
for and seize the tools used to facilitate the crime.

THE FENCE

The demand for stolen goods requires the thieves have access to an easy method of introducing it back into the marketplace. A fence or fencing operation is a common adjunct for disposing of stolen merchandise. A fence is commonly defined as an individual or organization that knowingly purchases illegally obtained or stolen goods for the purpose of placing those goods back into the marketplace. Identification, investigation, and apprehension of the fence or fencing method are the keys to reducing the threat from organized retail theft groups. Without an avenue for quick disposal of stolen merchandise the thieves are required to store the goods for longer periods of time which can increase their potential exposure to law enforcement. Additionally, self fencing requires the ORT members to actually dispose of the merchandise themselves which usually requires face-to-face transactions or internet sales which are increasingly easy to trace.

There are varying attributes and characteristic of fencing operations but they typically fall into one of the following categories:

Professional fences-These are commonly business owners who run legitimate businesses which serve as a front for the re-sale of stolen merchandise. They may advertise themselves as business wholesalers or re-sellers of goods and may have sophisticated, warehouse based operations. Professional fences may also operate 'cleaning' operations. Cleaning operations remove store labels or stickers and security tags and repackage stolen goods so they appear as though they came directly from a legitimate wholesaler or manufacturer. Once 'cleaned' the goods may then be sold to the public. The example in the Introduction of Rosemont Wholesale in Hayward, CA is a classic example of a professional fence. The Rosemont Wholesale operation employed multiple product cleaners to remove expiration or identification information and had a prominent internet presence. Although rare, the disruption of a professional fencing operation can have wide reaching consequences for a tremendous number of retails over a large geographic area. When the demand for stolen merchandise dries up so does the motivation to steal.

Professional fences can be identified through common investigative methods such as surveillance. As noted previously, Rosemont Wholesale was discovered by loss prevention agents who followed boosters out of their stores to the local fencing operation. The local fencing operation then resold the transported the merchandise to Rosemont for re-sale.   In retrospect Rosemont Wholesale was also easily identifiable based on their internet presence which offered a wide range on commonly stolen consumer goods and other items including bulk lots of jewelry. Rosemont Wholesale also had a multi-year history of suspicious financial transaction reporting by the financial institutions used by the owner. The suspicious cash withdrawals and deposits were quickly identified by the banks as being out of character for a wholesale business but were not detected by federal law enforcement for years.

Part-time fences-Part-time fences are also commonly business owners who derive a portion of their profits from retailing stolen goods.   These businesses may include pawnshops, convenience stores, neighborhood markets or liquor stores, appliance repair shops, and second hand stores.   Another common method for disposing of stolen merchandise for part-time fences is through flea markets and swap meets. These venues provide an area where bargain minded shoppers may be willing to turn a blind eye towards suspect merchandise in exchange for substantially discounted prices. Flea markets and swap meets also provide fences with an opportunity to dispose of damaged merchandise which cannot be resold or returned to legitimate merchants.

Part-time fences can be at the same time be easier and more difficult than other fencing operations to identify. The fact that they have a static business location makes them more susceptible to identification by local law enforcement and retail loss prevention agents. However, stolen merchandise can be easily intermingled with legitimately purchased goods making it difficult to identify. In the Rosemont Whole investigation, surveillance revealed boosters entering neighborhood stores carrying large garbage bags and multiple boxes but leaving empty handed.

Neighborhood hustlers/The Trunk Salesman-These bottom feeding opportunistic fences use simple street hustling techniques in an effort to rapidly move smaller quantities of stolen goods. These fences are sometimes encountered by law enforcement as a result of calls for service and are usually found in shopping mall parking lots and other areas with high pedestrian traffic. There is an unfortunate mindset among some law enforcement agencies which regards these fences as a nuisance problem, unworthy of investigation. However, the experience of some seasoned investigators is that these fences are commonly involved in multiple economic crimes of opportunity involving counterfeit goods, narcotics trafficking, and possession of stolen property from residential burglaries. Allowing these street level fences to operate creates the impression of a permissive environment when it comes to certain 'non-violent' crimes. Additionally, these 'street fences' may also act as an intermediary to larger fencing operations either by retailing stolen goods or acquiring goods to be passed on to the higher echelon fence.

Drug Dealers-Many drug users do not have the ability to pay their dealers in cash so they frequently will barter drugs for high value consumables such as tobacco, liquor, and meat. Law enforcement officers who encounter the apprehended lower level drug addicted booster frequently presume the theft occurred for personal use. After all, who really wants to eat a steak that was pulled out of someone's pants? However, it is more common that the drug addict will forgo consumption of the stolen goods and instead attempt to exchange them for drugs. Some dealers will provide their customers with lists of acceptable goods they will take in exchange for the drugs. These goods are either personally used by the dealer, self fenced such as through parking lot sales, or sold or transferred to upper level professional fences.

Amateurs-Amateurs fence for personal use or gain. They may retail these items to friends and family while operating out of their houses or use internet sites. Amateur fences should not be discounted simply because they traffic in low volume, low value goods. Depending on their successes in their early stages, amateur fences may advance to a more sophisticated level.

INTERNET

A prevalent trend used by all level of fences and many ORT groups is internet fencing using several well known online marketplaces such as eBay and Craigslist. According to some retailer estimates, approximately 18% of stolen goods are fenced on the internet. Additionally, a study by the National Retail Federation, 66% of surveyed retailers reported they were able to identify or recover stolen merchandise being fenced online. The process of disposing of stolen merchandise over the internet has been termed 'e-fencing.'

E-fencing has several benefits for ORT groups including anonymity, expanded reach, and increased profitability. Unlike traditional face-to-face fencing operations, Internet auction and consumer sites provide the perception of anonymity. Users of sites like eBay and Craigslist are identified only by a self generated user name and geographical region. A single user can operate multiple difference user names simultaneously in order to expand their operation and confuse investigators. Retail loss prevention agencies commonly have difficulty obtaining information from these providers as they will not divulge customer information without a court order, search warrant or subpoena.

An e-fencing operation has greater reach than a traditional storefront or flea market fencing operation. An e-fence can offer their stolen merchandise in any geographic area they choose and they are not limited to drawing customers from a particular locality. Another aspect which increases the reach of the e-fence is their ability to market their goods 24 hours a day whereas a traditional fencing operation is usually limited to quasi normal business hours. These factors provide the e-fence with a distinct advantage over traditional fencing operations.

Most importantly, e-fences are able to increase their revenue by selling stolen goods online. The profit margin on stolen merchandise fenced over the internet is typically much higher than merchandise told through a traditional fence. E-fenced merchandise can often be sold for approximately 70% of its retail value. Compared to traditional fencing operations which commonly sell stolen merchandise for approximately 30-50% of its retail price, e-fencing affords ORT rings for the potential for higher profit margins. This may be due in to the fact that during face-to-face purchases of stolen goods, the consumer is able to recognize the questionable legality of the merchandise and are subsequently willing to pay less for items in physical markets than online.

Identification of e-fencing operations is relatively easy. Suspect fences can be identified and monitored based on the types and quantities of goods they sell. It is difficult to imagine the circumstances which would lead someone to having over purchased 20 boxes of smoking cessation products, cases of high end razor blades, or multiple containers of different baby formula products. Both law enforcement and loss prevention agents should attempt to identify e-fencing operations by searching for keywords associated with commonly stolen goods. Particular attention should be paid to those offering multiple items of identical products as "NIB" or "new in box" items or goods.

People are creatures of habit, including e-fences. They do not tend to spend a lot of time writing different varieties of advertising for their products and persistent review of relevant keywords will quickly reveal the use of repeated phrases, words, and images used by e-fences to list their wares.

Another easy way to identify e-fenses looking at the 'wanted to buy' postings in addition to the retail or 'for sale' postings. There are not many legitimate businesses which offer to buy diabetic test strips with "no questions asked."

EBAY

eBay is one of the largest online marketplaces and has taken a number of steps designed to prevent the sale of stolen merchandise on their site. In 2008 eBay began an aggressive program to address the sales of stolen merchandise on their site by creating their PROACT program. This program provides retailers with an avenue to quickly submit and receive information on eBay sellers suspected of trafficking stolen merchandise. eBay's investigators can also assist loss prevention departments by providing undercover accounts to purchase suspected stolen merchandise, analytical support in linking confirmed e-fences to other users and accounts, and suspending the accounts of identified fencing operations.

Other efforts by eBay to curb the sale of stolen merchandise through their site include:

The restriction of certain items included those that are federally regulated such as firearms, tobacco, and alcohol and others. eBay's list of prohibited items is fairly comprehensives and includes a variety of other restricted, but not prohibited, commonly stolen goods including baby formula, cosmetics, and over the counter medications, eBay does not ban the sale of these items, but requires enhanced descriptions of expiration dates.

The provision of a "Report Item" link on every product page which provides an avenue for reporting a listing violation, including stolen property. However, retailers are required to affirm the listed item is stolen which can be difficult without identifying specific serial numbers or marking which are usually not visible from the posting page or accompanying photos.

eBay will also create "exception reports" for PROACT member retailers. These reports can help identify retailers of common stolen products from a retailer's stores based on pricing, quantities sold, and high-theft areas. Once generated, these reports can provide retail loss prevention agents with information regarding the top suspicious sellers of high risk items for use in target operations and investigations to determine if the goods are in fact stolen and being fenced on eBay.

eBay also has created a number of tools and instituted a number of policies designed to provide law enforcement with access to relevant information. eBay has a designated Law Enforcement portal, located at https://lers.corp.ebay.com, which allows investigators to request information from eBay about specific users suspected of violating various types of crimes. These criminal violations can include eBay or PayPal account takeovers, child exploitation investigations, counterfeiting and intellectual property crimes, seller or buyer fraud, identity theft, illegal items including stolen goods, money laundering, terrorism, and vehicle theft.

The sign up and vetting process are very easy and allows law enforcement to submit information requests and legal demands (search warrants, court orders, and subpoenas) through the site. eBay attempts to respond promptly to all requests and legal demands and can provide the following information regarding listings:

User Registration Information-ID History, Financial Info, and Billing History

Listing Information-All Items Listed, All Items Won, Item Details, Seller Registration Information, and Buyer Registration Information

In order to obtain eBay information you must provide them with either:

The eBay User ID which is a minimum four character, alpha or alphanumeric series of characters which identify the user. For example stolen_goods123. There are no spaces in the eBay user ID.

The eBay Item Number is a 10-13 digit number associated with the item such as 9910111213141

The eBay Email Address

Information regarding users of eBay's PayPal system can include:

eBay and PayPal

Subscriber Information

Financial Instruments

Transactional Data

Internet Protocol (IP) Addresses

Buyer complaint data

To search for records associated with a PayPal account or transaction you will need to provide the company with a legal demand and any of the following suspect identification information:

The PayPal Email Address

The PayPal Account Number which is a 19 digit number with no spaces

The PayPal Transaction ID, an alpha numeric sequence at least five characters long. If the sequence begins with the codes QQI, QQE, QQW, QQC, or QQA, the three preceding letters need to be removed when submitting via the law enforcement portal.

In addition to the services offered to retail investigators and law enforcement officials, eBay has also implemented a number of procedures designed to vet seller information and allow consumers to proactively identify suspicious listings, including:

Enhanced seller vetting-eBay verifies users' names, address, and phone numbers and limits the activity of new sellers until such time as the seller builds a good business record on the site.

Filtering-eBay utilizes a number of filers to search for suspicious listings. These filters automatically look for anomalies in the seller's financial, user, or feedback information. The filters also scan item categories for certain keywords and prices to identify suspicious postings.

Internal exception reporting-eBay runs a number of internal reports on multiple high risk and commonly stolen categories including gift cards, health and beauty products, and baby formula. These reports are designed to identify high volume sellers in high theft categories for further review or internal monitoring.

Payment holds-Through eBay's financial services arm, PayPal, eBay institutes a 21 day hold on funds in new accounts effectively freezing the funds until the hold expires. eBay uses this as a deterrent to those who would list stolen items online to prevent ORT, boosters, and other criminals from quickly converting stolen goods into cash.

Messaging-eBay reminds sellers of certain product types about their rules respective to those items such as listing expiration dates of perishable items in the advertisement. This is seen as a method to product the purchaser and to dissuade sellers of stolen goods by notifying them the items they are selling are under increased scrutiny by eBay.

CRAIGSLIST

Craigslist is quickly becoming one of the 'go-to' websites to fence stolen property over the internet. Similar to the classified advertisements section in a newspaper, Craigslist has no involvement in the actual transaction other than the actual posting itself. Craigslist does not charge for postings in the 'for sale' categories, nor does it make any money from a completed transaction.

The same degree of registration and vetting are not required in order to post on Craigslist and the site does not collect the same type of information required by other sites. Craigslist has also created the appearance of a more permissive environment for illegal activity, such as posting stolen property, as evidenced by a less rigid set of restricted items. E-fences are attracted to Craigslist by the higher degree of anonymity afforded them, and a less regulated environment, as opposed to other sites like eBay.

Craigslist's subpoena compliance and corporate security departments are notorious for their quick response to legal demands but they do not seem to have them same proactive mechanism in place, such as the automated filters or description requirements of eBay, designed to deter fencing operations. Craigslist posts approximately 1 million 'for sale' postings every month and its 30 plus employees are unable to monitor or review even a small fraction of the advertisements. Craigslist relies on site users to utilize the flagging feature found on every posting to identify suspect postings. Once an unspecified number of flags are received the company will pull the posting but it is unclear and highly unlikely, they take any further action at that point. Upon receipt of appropriate legal process, Craigslist is able to provide some captured digital information such as the internet protocol (IP) address of the computer used to generate the posting and email and phone numbers provided by the user.

Additionally, as Craigslist does not have an integrated remittance system such as PayPal, they inherently have a diminished ability to collect certain types of information such as financial data. Remittances on Craigslist are handled in whatever manner the buyer and seller agree to whether it's cash payments during a face to face meeting or using other payment services such as Western Union. The lack of controls over individual postings in high risk categories and an inability to collect the same information as other retailers is causing Craigslist to effectively become an internet black market.

SELF FENCING-GIFT CARDS

Self fencing using gift cards is another emerging trend used by ORT rings to convert stolen merchandise into cash. In an effort to reduce the amount of fraud associated with returns of stolen merchandise, many retailers have moved away from exchanging returned items for cash. Instead they will offer to credit the account used to purchase the items or offer store credit in exchange. ORT rings who use or specialize in return fraud and counterfeit receipts have figured out an easy way to exploit the return policies of some of the major retailers by exchanging stolen goods for gift cards. Gift cards are offered by many large retailers in lieu of cash when the returned item in not accompanied by a receipt and when the customer did not use a credit card to purchase the goods. These gift cards easily portable and anonymous which has led to development of a secondary market where the cards can be exchanged for cash.

There has been a proliferation of internet based and retail gift card exchange services which allow legitimate customers and ORT crews to exchange their cards for those of other merchants or receive a percentage of the value of the card in cash. These exchange and redemption services offer between 50-70% of the value of the card and make their profit by retailing the cards for 70-90% of their value. These services allow booster rings to easily convert their stolen merchandise into gift cards and then convert or redeem their gift cards into cash bypassing traditional fences and financial institutions. In some instances the cards are retailed directly through internet marketplaces such as eBay and Craigslist.

THE INVESTIGATION

There are several law enforcement stakeholders in ORT investigations, each with its own strengths and limitations. State and local law enforcement are routinely involved in investigating property crimes, including retail theft. Local law enforcement may come into contact with these criminals as a result of variety of activities including apprehension of suspects by retail loss prevention agents, encountering the suspicious possession of large amounts of retails products during routine calls for service or traffic stops, through other investigations such as narcotics, while addressing problematic businesses or establishments, or through proactive measure such as motel sweeps. Because of their frequent contact with these types of cases and suspects, state and local law enforcement agencies usually have a better chance of recognizing professional thieves and have a greater understanding of local criminal activity. Additionally, local law enforcement agencies are usually more adept at recruiting informants using the same successful techniques used to target street and mid-level narcotics trafficking. Local law enforcement efforts are investigating and prosecuting ORT may be hampered by limited resources and higher priorities in their jurisdiction such as gangs and drugs. Consequently, property crimes, including ORT are commonly given low priority in many areas.

However, the multijurisdictional issues inherent in ORT investigations are often the purview and expertise of federal law enforcement agencies. The federal law enforcement agencies have defined, but in the case of ORT investigations, frequently overlapping jurisdictional responsibilities based on the crime under investigation. For example, the FBI has primary responsibility for investigating the interstate transportation of stolen property, terrorism, and organized crime groups, ICE has responsibility for investigating money laundering, intellectual property crimes investigations, and cross-border transactions, the Secret Service has responsibility for certain types of fraud and counterfeiting cases, not just US currency, and the IRS has jurisdiction over fraudulent tax returns and failure to report income. Federal law enforcement agencies also bring assets and resources to the table which most local law enforcement agencies to not possess including the ability to task other field offices in different states to follow-up investigative leads and a depth of experience investigating complex conspiracy crimes. Specific examples of federal law enforcement's investigation into ORT include the following agencies and their respective resources and responsibilities:

FBI-The FBI operates several major theft task forces in large metropolitan areas including multi-jurisdictional task forces comprised of federal, state, and local law enforcement representatives in Miami, El Paso, New York, Memphis, and Chicago. These groups are responsible for all categories of major theft including cargo theft, interstate vehicle theft rings, high value collectibles such as art, jewelry, and gemstones, as well as, organized retail theft rings. Ironically, despite their reputation as one of the preeminent law enforcement agencies in the world, the FBI still relies upon retailers to identify ORT rings and patterns and initiates the investigation until it warrants their involvement. This may be due, in part, to the fact that other organized theft activities with greater economic impact, including cargo theft and interstate vehicle theft, draw the majority of their resources. The FBI is also likely hampered by the fact that many of its criminal investigators were reassigned to counterterrorism investigation post 9/11, drawing resources from other traditional criminal investigations.

ICE-ICE has increased their presence in traditional criminal investigations, including ORT, where the crime relates to money laundering, exporting of stolen goods, or involves crimes committed by illegal aliens. ICE does has started intelligence gathering on ORT in several specific threat areas including New York, Miami, Los Angeles, and Houston but does not have dedicated ORT task forces. ICE will involve themselves in those types of cases when one of the other underlying crimes is violated or suspected of being violated. For example, ICE would not routinely involve themselves in an ORT investigation but would if the boosters were known to be illegal immigrants specifically brought into the country to commit thefts. Similarly, a fencing operation would be targeting for money laundering violations and not the underlying Specified Unlawful Activity (SUA) of interstate transportation of stolen property.

But law enforcement are not the only agencies involved in investigating ORT. The retailers have a vested interest in the investigation and prosecution of organized theft rings. These retail loss prevention departments have regular exposure to these types of crimes and criminals. Loss prevention departments are also in communication with other branches of the same store chain and may possess information and intelligence which local, state, and federal law enforcement agencies do not. Furthermore, some retail loss prevention departments are well funded and equipped and are able to conduct external surveillance and investigations. Larger agencies also have the ability to acquire product for use in sting operations targeting ORT rings and fencing operations. The lack of peace officer powers is a double edged sword in the loss prevention world. While some exclusive peace officer powers, such as the ability to execute search warrants, are unavailable to loss prevention agents, they are also not bound by some requirements and regulations such as giving a suspect their Miranda rights before interrogation.

One of the key components to initiating a successful ORT investigation is partnering with the respective agencies and organization with investigative mandate, resources, and information and intelligence to link cross jurisdictional cases. No one entity possesses all of the tools necessary to conduct a comprehensive ORT investigation and prosecution and it takes a multi-disciplinary approach to dismantle these groups. However, it is unrealistic to expect all of these agencies will bring their respective resources to bear on every crime. In addition to resource limitations, many jurisdictions have statutory or internal requirements or thresholds which must be met in order to justify allocating resources to address a particular problem. For example, California law enforcement agencies are limited to arresting and prosecuting felony theft cases unless the value of the goods exceeds $950. Sophisticated boosters are aware of this limit and will endeavor to try to limit their thefts to values under that amount in case they are apprehended. However, the California penal code also allows for the arrest and prosecution for the felony crime of burglary in the investigation reveals the suspect purposefully entered a business with the intent to commit a theft. While there is no explicit threshold for federal involvement in ORT cases, there usually must be a substantial economic loss or other underlying issue in order for them to get involved. Many federal agencies have an unofficial threshold which requires more than $100,000 material loss, greater than $100,000 in laundered money or tax liability, other issues which substantially involve the investigative mandate of the respective agency. For example, if an al-Qaeda operative were caught stealing a pack of gum there is no doubt the FBI would involve themselves in the investigation. Similarly, an ORT ring with links to a gang or a drug trafficking organization would likely gain increased attention from federal law enforcement.

RESPONDING

The initial response of local law enforcement to calls for service that involve in-progress theft activity is a key step in laying the foundation for a successful ORT investigation. That means the first responding law enforcement officer holds the keys to the successful apprehension and investigation of the larger organization. However, proper response and investigation are not routinely taught to line level police officers. Preparation and planning are considered for many high-risk, but infrequent, crimes such as bank robbery, but the same efforts are not placed into the response and apprehension of retail thieves. The experiences of successful patrol officers in the apprehension of retail thieves, including professional boosters, indicate the following tactics should be considered:

Refrain from immediately entering the store or mall immediately if the crime is still in progress. The key to successful apprehension is establishing surveillance in parking lots or garages with an angle of observation which covers the logical exits. While it is hard to remain undetected in a black and white patrol car, responding officers should be cognizant of the fact professional boosters operate in groups and may have lookouts or drivers strategically positioned to observe responding officers and assist with the thief's escape. While responding, law enforcement officers should be alert to people who are sitting in vehicles near the exits of the targeting store. As noted previously, professional boosters prefer larger vehicles with greater storage capacity for stolen merchandise and the ability to transport multiple members of the group. Anomalies to look for include people sitting in vehicles where the outside conditions would normally dictate the vehicle be running in order to operate the air conditioning or heater. The booster's driver will attempt to avoid attention by leaving the engine off and avoiding visible exhaust or engine noises.

Depending on departmental policy, attempt to establish direct communications with the reporting party. Frequently, these are the loss prevention agents who are coordinating the in-store surveillance and apprehension teams and may be able to provide near real-time intelligence via closed circuit television cameras (CCTC). Some jurisdictions have radio systems which allow for tactical channels to be set up between responding officers and loss prevention agents and security officers. Professional boosters may be equipped with scanners, or scanner applications for smart phones, which serves to alert them to the law enforcement response. Direct communication via cellular phone reduces the potential for a coordinated law enforcement response to be detected.

A booster ring's mule, or the person who carries the stolen merchandise from the store to a vehicle, will commonly walk past their vehicle to see if they are being surveilled. The U-turn or 'crazy Ivan' is a counter surveillance tactic designed to alert the mule to the approach of store security and/or law enforcement without giving up the location of their vehicle.

Many booster and mules do not keep the keys to the vehicle on their possession. As with the counter surveillance tactics, they are attempting to avoid law enforcement from discovering their vehicle. The intended vehicle may be identified based on the preferences of many ORT rings towards larger vehicles, any obvious rental vehicles, and the observation of stolen merchandise in plain view. Additionally, booster vehicles may actually be identified after hours abandoned in the parking lot as the other members of the ring will usually flee via alternative transportation methods if one member is arrested.

Don't forget officer safety. Always presume there are other members of the group nearby. Many officers get caught up the mundane shoplifter in-custody and lower their guard on these 'routine' calls. A notorious example of the lengths some people are willing to go to attempt to free someone from a petty theft charge occurred on the night of March 7, 2003, Ukiah Police Department Sgt. Marcus Young responded to a local Wal-Mart to arrest a shoplifter. During the arrest, Sgt. Young was approached by the shoplifter's boyfriend, a violent felon, who pulled a gun and shot Sgt. Young five times.

INVESTIGATING

While there are a number of ways to proactively identify ORT and theft rings through the investigation of fencing operations, the most common opportunity comes when a booster is arrested by loss prevention or law enforcement. Once a professional booster has been identified there are several investigative steps which should be taken to order to differentiate the suspect as a professional thief as opposed to a casual shoplifter. These steps can help not only with prosecution, but also with the investigation of the larger organization.

There is a narrow window of opportunity to initiate these investigations. Apprehended suspects are vulnerable to debriefing for only a limited amount of time. Once contact is initiated with other members of the group their resistance to interrogation can increase. Physical evidence which may be located near the scene of the crime can be disposed of or moved by other members of the ORT team. The arrest of one member of the group may cause the remaining members to evacuate the area until the 'heat' is off.

INTERVIEWING/DEBRIEFING

The greatest opportunity to obtain incriminating information from the suspect and detailed intelligence regarding the organization of a booster ring or fencing operation is when a suspect is apprehended. In-custody professional thieves are susceptible to interrogation immediately after their arrest and can provide information about the techniques and tactics used by a criminal organization, how merchandise and locations are targets, and information regarding the fencing operation. Even though these are commonly lower level members of the larger ORT ring their value as potential sources of information should not be discounted.

Depending on the sophistication of the loss prevention department who affects the arrest, they may initiate an interrogation prior to notifying law enforcement. There are several benefits to this including the fact that civilian security representatives are not required to issue Miranda admonishments to apprehended suspects. However, one significant downside to private party interrogation is that some loss prevention departments do not record their interviews and only memorialize the suspect's answers in a written report.

Obtaining incriminating statements from a suspect and developing useful information from an interrogation is a critical component in any investigation whether performed by law enforcement officials or a retailer's loss prevention department. While complete instruction in effective interrogation techniques are outside the purview of this manual, it is usually most effective to begin a line of questioning regarding the crime under investigation once the suspect has already started answering questions. A common technique is to ask standard biographical questions which the suspect expects to be asked followed by specific questions about the crime. Once a criminal has answered a series of questions such as name, date of birth, and address, they have already been conditioned to answer. The critical point in any interrogation is the transition from these 'routine' questions into specific, often incriminating, information about the crime. An effective interview is planned in advance and designed to elicit not only statements which may be used against the criminal, but also provide investigators with intelligence about the larger organization. Using a standardized set of questions can help guide questioning, as well as, provide incriminating information for use by the prosecution, as well as, subsequent law enforcement and private industry investigations. Some examples of standardized interview questions which are designed to elicit useful information include:

Have you been arrested in the past ten years? How many times have you been caught shoplifting?

[This question appears to be a standard booking or interview question but helps to establish prior criminal acts. It also asks how many times the suspect has been caught stealing. This is an important distinction as some retailers do not contact law enforcement if their internal guidelines, such as total dollar amount of stolen goods, are not met. These detentions by store security would not routinely show up in criminal records information systems, but the suspect does not know this. Also, note the referral to the crime as shoplifting and not theft or stealing. This can help lower the suspect's guard into believing they are being interviewed about a petty crime and not a more serious offense. As discussed previously, many believe shoplifting is a separate, lesser offense and are more likely to discuss the specifics than if they were being questioned about stealing, organized retail theft, or burglary.]

Are you currently on probation or parole? If so, what for?

[Prior convictions and/or incarceration can be critical factors for evaluation by prosecutors, particularly if the prior crimes were theft related. Experienced criminal are conditioned to answer this question as they know it is easily verifiable by law enforcement. In an effort to appear cooperative, probationers and parolees will commonly disclose their supervised release status. This conditioned response sets the tone for other questions.]

Are you employed? If so, by who?

[This helps establish the crime(s) as a primary, or sole, source of income and differentiates the casual thief from a professional booster. It is an ideal transition question because it appears to be an innocuous question following the standard biographical or 'booking' questions. However, the transition from routine questioning to specific information and intelligence questioning begins at this point.]

Where are you staying?

[This question is not the same as 'What is your address?' and should be asked well after the initial biographical questioning. Many criminals have a memorized address they can recite to law enforcement. This address is sometimes a previous address, a post office box or private mail box, or, rarely, a family member's address. They will avoid giving a true location at all costs as they fear the search of their residence and/or alerting their family members about the continuing criminal acts. This question asks where the suspect is presently residing and can give investigators valuable information regarding the location of stolen merchandise and other co-conspirators. If their present accommodations are geographically different from their address, this may also indicate the suspect travelled in order to arrive in the city where the crime occurred. This inferred travel can be expanded upon later to identify the reasons and methods the suspect travelled to a particular area and may be an indicator of an ORT ring.]

How did you get here today?

[Usually, the suspect will respond with 'I got a ride from a friend.' This question is designed to illustrate the fact the suspect is acting in concert with someone else or identify the fact the suspect or their co-conspirators have a vehicle in the immediate vicinity. If the suspect has car keys in their possession, an attempt should be made to immediately locate it and secure it for further investigation.

Why do you shoplift?

[You can probably expect an answer of 'I don't know' but many thieves will try to minimize their crimes by attempting to give a sympathetic inducing excuse such as 'To feed my family.' However, if a suspect admits to stealing items which do not readily lend themselves to immediate consumption, they have set themselves up to answer questions identifying the ORT ring and/or fencing operation. It is difficult to justify stealing 30 pairs of designer jeans as a method of feeding one's family.]

When did you start shoplifting?

[This question also helps to differentiate the professional booster from a casual criminal. It can also help to open a line of questioning regarding how the suspect was recruited into an ORT ring.]

Is shoplifting a source of income?

[A follow-on to the preceding questions. If the suspect states they are a student or unemployed, they must have a source of income for routine expenses. If the suspect denies shoplifting is a source of income the interviewer may choose to either elaborate on the series of questions or defer it for later in the interview.]

What type of merchandise do you usually shoplift? Why?

[Identifying the fact that the suspect specifically targets certain items to steal may indicate they are a member of a professional ORT ring. The questions may also reveal the presence of 'shopping lists' or other preferences for goods which are specifically targeted for theft. The directions given to the booster regarding what to steal can help during investigations of the hierarchy of the group and assist loss prevention departments identify goods which may need a higher degree of security.]

Are you told to steal specific merchandise? If yes, what for and by who?

[As above, the specific targeting of merchandise for theft can provide valuable information for investigating law enforcement agencies and loss prevention agents. The fact that a booster was directed to steal specific merchandise illustrates they entered the business with the intent to steal (an element of the crime of burglary in some jurisdictions), the presence of an ORT ringleader who specifies which items should be stolen, and also provides valuable information regarding the targeting of high value items for loss prevention agents.]

What stores do you usually shoplift from? What stores do you avoid? Why?

[The acknowledgement that a booster targets specific stores and specifically avoids other retailers shows a level of sophistication missing from a casual thief. The answers can also provide further intelligence into the methods of operations of specific ORT rings.]

Is there a store you prefer to shoplift from? Why?

[This follow-on question is designed to elicit more information regarding method of operation.]

How many stores in a day/week/month do you shoplift from?

[This question, and the following questions, are designed to provide information for further investigation, aid prosecution by proving the suspect is a professional thief, and provide intelligence for retail loss prevention departments.]

How many days a week do you shoplift?

How much do you steal each time?

How much money do you make?

What do you do with the merchandise you shoplift? Sell it to a fence? Sell over the Internet? Refund to retailer? Sell at flea market? Street?

[Gaining insight into how the suspect disposes of the merchandise can help identify fencing operations, as well as, provide intelligence regarding local methods and techniques for disposing of stolen property.]

What happens to the merchandise after you sell it?

[Identification of the methods of disposing stolen property can lead to fencing operations and help expose the ORT hierarchy.]

What is the name of the individual and/or business the property is sold to?

[An individual booster may not have direct contact with the fencing operation but they are probably aware of how the merchandise is disposed of.]

How are they contacted?

[Invariably the fence is contacted, or contacts the booster ring, via cellular phone. This question can assist law enforcement officers with the legal justification for searching a suspect's cellular phone incident to their arrest or seeking a search warrant to search the phone.]

Do they own or operate a business?

[The identification of storefront or other retail operations can assist subsequent investigations into the fencing operation.]

Where do you take the merchandise? Storage locker? Pawn shop? Shipping agent, such as FedEx or UPS? An individual or business? An internet marketplace such as eBay or Craigslist?

[Locating where stolen merchandise is currently located, such as storage lockers or motel rooms can be a time sensitive issue. Many ORT rings will dissolve the operation in a particular locality if one member is apprehended. Additionally information about fencing operations can also be obtained by asking questions about the disposal of stolen merchandise.]

Does this individual know the property they are buying is stolen?

[Statements from the suspect can be used in subsequent investigations and prosecutions to establish the fact the fence was aware, or suspected, the goods were stolen; an essential element in proving the crime of possession of stolen property.]

How long have you been taking merchandise to the person/business?

[This is also designed to elicit information which may be useful in future investigation or prosecutions of fencing operations.]

How were you introduced to this person/business?

[Interactions with the fence may be handled by upper level members of sophisticated ORT rings. Lower level boosters may deal directly with the fence or their middleman.]

How are you paid for your merchandise?

[In most cases you would expect the booster is paid in cash. However, many steal to support drug habits and the exchange of narcotics for stolen property can elevate a simple petty theft investigation into a narcotics case.]

How many people do you usually work with? What are their roles?

[If the suspect is still talking at this point, they may be willing to answer further questions about the makeup and organization of the ORT ring. However, this question may put a suspect on the defensive as they are aware subsequent questions will ask to identify their co-conspirators. The interrogator may have to overcome substantial resistance on the part of the suspect as the other members of the group may be family members or close associates. Additionally, the suspect may fear retaliation for revealing the identities of others and refuse to answer this or related questions. Conversely, a criminal with no association to the other members of the group will frequently readily give up whatever information they possess in order to show their willingness to cooperate, diminish their role in the criminal organization, and attempt to broker a better deal for themselves.]

How do you communicate with other members of the group?

[This will usually be via cellular phone and text messages. Ask what names they are stored under in the suspect's phone. Once the names or monikers have been identified, ask for consent to search the phone to retrieve the phone numbers.]

How do you travel?

[This question is a follow-up to the earlier 'How did you get here today?' The answer to this question will reveal a lot about the suspect. It may establish the fact the criminal's vehicle is still parked in the area, or show they travelled from out of state for the purposes of committing crimes. Transportation related intelligence is critical in that it shows the sophistication of the group and also provides a method for tracing the means and source of payment for travel related services such as rental cars, bus tickets, and airline tickets.]

Who in the group handles the money? What do they do with it?

[Depending on the suspect's role in the ORT ring, they may or may not know the answer to this question. Lower level boosters and mules will be purposefully excluded from the financial aspects of the organization. However, they may have a general idea how much money the group generates and they will certainly know how much they are paid.]

INFORMANT RECRUITMENT

As with interview and interrogation, the full breadth of information regarding recruiting and handling informants is outside the purview of this manual. However, there are some basic steps which can be taken initially to make subsequent attempts at debriefing and recruiting the suspect easier. The first, and often times best, opportunity to recruit an ORT suspect generally occurs during the post arrest/post apprehension phase. The suspect is usually off centered, unnerved, frightened, and/or confused. They are separated from other members of the group and they may feel abandoned by them. The suspect may not have invoked their Miranda rights to stay silent or request representation by an attorney. The offender feels an immediate need to avoid incarceration and prosecution and they have immediate actionable intelligence which they can trade. All of these factors are usually diminished over time. After the initial apprehension, the suspect may have contact with other members of the ORT ring who may reassure them, threaten them, or provide support including bail money or legal representation. The more time that passes, the less value the informant's information has. Additionally, the prosecution may drop or reduce the initial charges. All of these factors combine to increase the importance of timely recruitment and debriefing of informants.

Most interviews and interrogations performed by asset protection members focus on obtaining a confession regarding the crime and often overlook the possibility of ORT involvement. If the suspect provides a confession, they are primed to be approached about providing other substantial assistance.   This approach can be made by civilian loss prevention personnel in exchange for declining to prosecute. Once law enforcement is involved the decision to offer cooperation as an option during the investigation and prosecution must be done with the knowledge and consent of the prosecutor. Seeking this knowledge and consent from the prosecutor can be one of the factors which substantially increase the time between the apprehension and arrest and the decision to become an informant. Anything that can be done to reduce that time increases the likelihood of a successful recruitment.

In order to obtain case consideration, a suspect must provide substantial assistance to the investigation. This includes:

A full confession and acknowledgment of guilt and responsibility

Surrendering all stolen goods, burglary tools, drugs, monies, weapons, and other contraband items

Identification of all co-conspirators including other boosters and fences

Providing accurate and truthful information-Minimization and deception can result in the exclusion of an informant

Cooperate with future investigations and testify if necessary.

Providing testimony in court can often times be a deal breaker with many informants. They are usually willing to provide information when they believe they can do so anonymously or with minimal chance of being discovered by their former co-conspirators. However, the prospect of testifying in open court is often enough to make even the most motivated informant re-think their willingness to cooperate. Many are willing to testify in exchange for relocation assistance but this is not usually offered by local jurisdictions and rarely is it an option in ORT cases. The requirement to testify should be carefully weighed against the value of the information they can provide versus the value of their potential future testimony.

There are two main approaches for recruiting informants immediately post apprehension-the hard sell and the long term approach. The hard sell is useful immediately after the arrest, when the suspect is most susceptible to recruitment. It is also useful if the charges the suspect was arrested for are considered minor, prosecution is doubtful, or if bail is likely to be low. The hard sell also offers the suspect immediate leniency in exchange for immediate actionable intelligence. Often, law enforcement will exchange leniency for information not relating to the crime the suspect was arrested for. For example if a booster is arrested by a retailers loss prevention agents and cannot or will not provide information regarding the members and operations of the ORT group, local law enforcement will often barter for other information such as narcotics and weapons.

The long term approach, sometimes referred to as planting the seed, is a much more refined process for recruiting informants and requires a higher level of skill and sophistication on the part of the investigator in order to be successful. It works by identifying the motivations and concerns of the suspect and offers them a long term strategy for getting out of their current predicament. Commonly, in conspiracy investigations, the apprehended suspect may have interpersonal problems with other members of the group such as envy, jealousy, or resentment. The long term approach plays to the suspect's motivations in order to accomplish the overall needs of the investigation. This method works well when the suspect is going to be incarcerated for a prolonged period of time, is facing charges with the possibility of lengthy incarceration, and faces a high bail. The longer the suspect has to ponder their fate, especially when there is a lack of support from other members of the ORT group, the more the seeds of discontentment will grow. Unfortunately, the information available to the suspect may be dated but they are usually more willing to provide complete information regarding other suspects and their methods of operation.

The following are some general guidelines for use in recruiting informants:

Develop rapport with the suspect-find common interests, topics, locations to begin to humanize you and lower the suspects guard. Be aware of sophisticated suspects attempting the same technique with you.

Conduct the interview in an area with minimum distractions but maximum control

Use no more than two interviewers/investigators

Make the offer succinctly. State the conditions clearly and unequivocally.

Pay attention to objections, fears, concerns, and reasons for rejection

Make a second attempt if the first attempt fails. Address any issues or concerns raised by the suspect and attempt to offer remedies or explanations.

THE CAR AUTOPSY

Getting an apprehended suspect to confess and debrief is a main method of obtaining incriminating information and intelligence regarding the operations of an ORT ring. Additionally, physical evidence such as tools or adjunct used by thieves such as booster boxes, bags, and EAS tag removers, or cutting instruments can be critical items of physical evidence. However, perhaps the greatest source of evidence and intelligence is the vehicle used by the suspect(s). Depending on the sophistication of the booster ring the vehicle may serve as the main method of transportation for the groups as they travel from city to city, be a temporary storage or staging area for stolen merchandise from other stores, and contain other evidence useful to investigators including the identity of the vehicle owner/renter, indicia of other storage locations, and indications of the location of other members of the group.

When investigating ORT it is essential to attempt to identify any vehicles used by the group, secure them promptly, and seek authorization to search via consent, probation, or a search warrant, and to consider the vehicle as an instrumentality of the crime and treat it accordingly.

Speed is critical in identifying the suspects' vehicle(s). Upon apprehension of one or more of the members of the group, the remaining boosters are likely to attempt to flee the area to avoid capture and to dispose of any merchandise they may have on them. Many booster rings have experienced the apprehension of one of their members before. They know statistically 50% of the time the loss prevention department will not notify law enforcement and will rely on internal policies of identification, reprimand, and release so the remaining members of the group may still be in the immediate area of the arrest and/or the vehicle. Suspect interviews indicates many times the keys are left inside the vehicle to prevent the other members of the ORT ring from being stranded upon the arrest of the one who had the keys. However, as the vehicle is often used to store merchandise when travelling between stores and/or cities the vehicle may be locked to prevent the thieves from having their merchandise stolen by other criminals. If an apprehended suspect is in possession of car keys an attempt should be made to immediately identify the vehicle and secure it. The two most common methods of identifying the suspect's vehicle is to review exterior video surveillance before the suspect entered the store or mall and driving the parking lots and surrounding areas while clicking the remote button on the key chain. Common vehicle used by booster rings tend towards being large sized SUVs, passenger or mini vans, and large sedans. Once identified, the vehicle should be secured while awaiting legal authority to search it. Remember, there is no expectation of privacy for items in plain view in a vehicle so the visible contents should be inspected without opening the doors.

SEARCH AUTHORITY

Standard search and seizure laws apply to the vehicles used by ORT rings. Unless there is a valid exception to Fourth Amendment, law enforcement officers are required to obtain a search warrant before entering the vehicle and attempting to recover evidence.

Consent-Most sophisticated boosters are going to deny dominion and control over a vehicle and are unlikely to give consent. However, this does not mean investigators should not ask for consent to search. If consent to search the vehicle is granted, it should be memorialized either in a signed waiver form or via audio or video recording.

Search Incident to Arrest-The United States Supreme Court limited the ability of law enforcement officers to search vehicles in a 2009 decision called US v. Gant. Many law enforcement agencies believed that vehicle searches were off limits incident to the arrest of the driver or occupant. However, what the courts specifically stated is that a search of the vehicle incident to arrest is permissible if the police are searching for evidence of the crime under investigation. For example, if a police officer stops a vehicle based on information provided to him/her from the loss prevention agents of a merchant, it is permissible to search the vehicle incident to the arrest of the suspect for evidence of the crime under investigation. In this case if they are under private persons arrest or being arrested by the officer for crimes related to ORT, the officer may search the vehicle for evidence of the crime such as stolen merchandise and burglary tools. This area of law is not entirely settled and it is critical to consult with a prosecuting attorney.

Probation/Parole-If an apprehended suspect is on probation or parole with a warrantless search clause as a condition of their release, their vehicle may be searched. In order for this type of search to withstand subsequent defense challenges, documentation of the affirmative link between the suspect and the vehicle is essential. This may be established through statements, physical evidence such as car keys or rental agreements, and video surveillance.

Private Party Searches-Private parties, such as asset protection agents, should not be used as agents of the police to conduct warrantless vehicle searches. If there are no other options available, seek a search warrant.

Search Warrant-Uniformed patrol officers are the most likely to encounter an ORT suspect. However, they are often inexperienced in the area of drafting search warrant affidavits. But a search warrant is the absolute best, most effective way to search a vehicle for evidence and gather intelligence regarding the larger conspiracy and should be pursued whenever possible. [Depending on page count, consider adding a sample search warrant to the Appendix]

VEHICLE CONTENT ANALYSIS

Using the techniques perfected in the post seizure analysis of vehicles used to smuggle narcotics can offer a valuable framework for searching for evidence and intelligence in a vehicle used by a booster ring. Sometimes referred to a vehicle content analysis, this process can assist with investigations where the suspects are not cooperative during the initial stages of the investigation. The analysis of the contents of a suspect's vehicle can aid in:

Intelligence gathering and lead development-Identifying contacts, telephone numbers, names, and addresses of co-conspirators and fences

Assist in obtaining information for use in subsequent search warrants

Interviews and Interrogations

Identification of other crimes/locations by determining routes of travel, prior locations visited, and the dates and times of those occurrences

The procedure of vehicle content analysis includes the following:

1) Collect everything-Collect all items in the vehicle including receipts, pieces of paper, or other written or printed information. Do not discount any particular piece of potential evidence at the time because it may become important later on. Most law enforcement officers do not want to collect the fast food bag with the partially eaten sandwich and the stale French fries but the receipt contained inside can be a valuable clue in determining prior locations or routes of travel. Items to be searched for and collected include, but should not be limited to:

Documents or papers with names, addresses, or phone numbers, including printed or electronic address books

Business cards

Maps or GPS devices

Identification documents and credit cards

Wire transfer receipts

Prepaid calling cards

Receipts for the maintenance or purchases related to the vehicle including gas receipts and highway toll receipts

Restaurant and fast food receipts

Indicia of stays at hotels/motels including keys, key cards, registration paperwork, and receipts

Any cellular phone or digital device capable of capturing, collecting, storing, displaying, receiving, or transmitting electronic data such as iPhones, iPods, iPads, laptop computers, etc.

Other papers, receipts, or financial records

2) Once collected, examine each item for investigative relevance. Items may be grouped together such as electronic devices, printed or written documents, and other items.

3) If necessary, use the dates and times found on any of the items to create a chronology of the suspect's or group's activities. This is sometimes known as time line development and may assist in developing further areas for investigations

including communicating with other jurisdictions regarding recent, possibly related, ORT activity.

4) Pursue all investigative leads. You are likely not reading a book about investigating organized retail theft if you were simply content to arrest someone and then walk away. Conspiracy investigations can be long, complex affairs. But it is through the initial investigation that the larger criminal organization can be revealed.

GPS

As many ORT rings travel between multiple destinations, they may use global positioning system (GPS devices) to help navigate between unfamiliar areas. Similar to computers and many cellular phones, these devices retain a considerable amount of data in their memory even if the history has been deleted. Using the proper forensic tools and techniques it is often possible to recover deleted information from these devices. This information can lead to storage locker locations, transitional housing used by the group such as hotels and motels, and may provide indications of other past, present, or future targeted jurisdictions.

PHONES

Cellular phones can be one of the most invaluable pieces of evidence recovered from a suspect or from their vehicle. Many criminals believe their use of prepaid cellular phone services such as Boost, Virgin Mobile, and MetroPCS makes them anonymous and untraceable. With respect to the identity of the subscriber this is partially true. However, the phones themselves can retain valuable information such as text messages, call logs, and image and video files of co-conspirators. Additionally, the call detail records (CDRs) maintained by the cellular service providers maintain transaction records of all incoming and outgoing phone calls. These records are available to law enforcement through the service of a search warrant, court order, or subpoena. It is unclear if these records are available to asset protection departments are they typically only requested if the corporation filed a civil lawsuit against the suspect and subpoenaed the records as part of the process.

Examination of a cellular phone seized pursuant to the arrest of a suspect by law enforcement is governed by the same rules that apply to other searches. They must be made with a valid

126

exception to the Fourth Amendment such as consent, probation, parole, exigent circumstances, or incident to the arrest, or they must be made pursuant to a search warrant. Many law enforcement agencies possess various tools and techniques for recovering data forensically from cellular phones. But this area of evidence and intelligence has largely gone unnoticed and unused by civilian asset protection departments. While it is not possible to cover all of the steps for a complete forensic examination of a cellular phone in this book, there are some general steps which can be taken to preserve existing evidence and prevent its destruction.

PRESERVING ELECTRONIC EVIDENCE

The first rule in dealing with a cellular phone seized incident to arrest or apprehension is to prevent the device from communicating with the cellular service network. No other form of evidence can be as quickly and easily destroyed remotely as the data on a cellular device. As long as the device is on and communicating with the network the possibility of unintentional or deliberate loss of evidence due to incoming calls or text messages exists. Additionally, a variety of methods exist for the remote deletion or some or all of the digital contents of a phone. Current recommendations regarding the seizure of a cellular phone dictate the phone be turned off in order to prevent the possibility of accidental or intentional deletion of evidence from the device. However, some users will program the security settings of the device to activate the handset security lock when the power is turned on. Circumventing or removing handset pass code locks is a field of forensics which is still evolving and it is not always possible to bypass the lock. If a forensic examination can be completed promptly, experts recommend leaving the device powered on as long as steps are taken to prevent the phone from communicating with the service network. If there is a delay in the examination it is recommended the device be turned off. If the device is going to be left on the following techniques may be used to prevent the device from communicating with the network.

PREVENTING THE PHONE FROM COMMUNICATING WITH THE NETWORK

There are several methods for preventing a device from communicating with the cellular service provider's network. Principally these methods rely on the use of an adjunct device or material to block the radio signal of the cell site from establishing a connection with the device. It is important to note that none of these methods have been studied scientifically and it is unlikely any given mechanical signal blocking method will be effective on 100% of cellular devices in the market and in every given situation. A cell phone with a full battery charge in close proximity to a cell tower may still establish a connection despite the best attempts to mechanically block the signal.

There is another factor to consider when using mechanical methods of signal blocking. A cellular phone not actively being used will issue a signal to the cell tower with which it has the strongest connection with every 10-30 seconds. This assists the cellular service provider in locating the device in the event of an incoming phone call, text message, or data event. When the device senses it does not have a connection with a cell tower, it begins to search for a signal at a much higher rate; in some cases as quickly as once per second. This increased activity by the cellular device can drain the battery many times faster than if the phone was in regular standby mode. Some of the methods discussed do not allow for a power cable to remain attached to the device while it is being protected from communicating with the network. The end result could be a dead battery when the phone appeared to have a full charge when placed inside the mechanical signal blocking method.

Turn it off-This is the easiest way to secure a device but it can come with a price. Some users may have enabled a handset security lock which engages when the phone is powered off and then back on again. Prior to turning the device off the investigator should attempt to preserve the evidence on the screen by using digital photographs or video. Turning the phone off may also result in a loss of information stored in the volatile memory of the phone.

Airplane Mode-One of the most effective methods for preventing a device from communicating with the network while maintaining the battery life is to place the phone into Airplane Mode. This feature allows the device to remain powered on but 'disconnects' the antenna of the device. The phone will not make or receive calls, text messages, emails, data events, GPS updates, or program updates while in this mode. The software programs and features of the phone which do not require interaction with the Internet or the cellular network will continue to work. It is possible to complete a forensic examination of the device while the phone is in Airplane Mode. The Airplane Mode feature can typically be found in the 'Setting' or 'Tools' menus of the device and sometimes in the 'Phone Settings' sub menu. Unfortunately, this only works on devices that do not have an activated handset security lock. Curiously, not every phone has Airplane Mode as a setting but the majority of phones currently in use are equipped with this option. It is important to note Airplane mode will not always disconnect the Wi-Fi function of the phone and it may need to be turned off separately.

Removing the SIM card-GSM or iDEN phones are equipped with SIM (Subscriber Identity Module) cards. Removing these cards from the phone prevents it from communicating with the network. A forensic examination may be conducted on the card which can reveal some information. However, an examination of the device will typically require the SIM card to be re-inserted. Several forensic companies offer the training and equipment necessary to program 'cloned' SIM cards.

132

These cards are manually programmed with the unique identification numbers of the original card. The manual programming does not include the encryption key necessary for the device to activate to the cellular network. This tricks the device into allowing it to operate as if the SIM card were present however it does not allow the device to communicate with the network. A forensic examination can be done without the possibility of evidence deletion caused by communication with the cellular network.

Faraday Bags-These reusable bags consist of several layers of metal mesh such as nickel, copper, and silver plated nylon mesh, which have radio frequency interference properties. The metals inside these bags attempt to block the signal communications between the mobile device's antenna and nearby cell tower. The costs of these bags can be cost prohibitive if they are to be used on every cell phone seized (approximately $25-30 each). You would not think the use of a bag would require the user to follow complicated instructions, and yet I have seen law enforcement officers consistently fail to use a Faraday bag appropriately. Unfortunately, the bag is opaque and it is impossible to tell if the signal is in fact completely blocked as you cannot see the screen while the device is inside the bag.

Metal Mesh-Several cell phone forensic training and equipment companies offer metal mesh for sale with radio frequency interference capabilities. One of the advantages of this material is that it semi-opaque which allows the user to still view the screen of the device and to determine whether the signal is in fact blocked. Also, it is possible to wrap the device and attached cable in the material and perform a forensic examination, including manipulating the keys and screen, while shielding the device from the network. The material is less expensive than the Faraday bags and can be re-used.

INTELLIGENCE AND INFORMATION SHARING

LRPNET

Information and intelligence sharing between public safety and private business entities is a critical component of both proactive and reactive investigations into ORT rings. There are several resources available to share information between agencies. Additionally, there are services and databases available which enable authorized law enforcement agencies access to near real time data to assist in the identification of suspicious businesses.

One highly touted information sharing resource is the Law Enforcement Retail Partnership Network (LERPNet). LERPNet was designed as a secure, nationwide database designed to allow reporting and information sharing of retail theft incidents. The initiative was developed as an offshoot of a FBI mandate to establish a task force and provide criminal investigation expertise to assist the retail community in the development of a private sector database for tracking ORT information. LERPNet is accessible to criminal investigators through the FBI's Law Enforcement Online (LEO) portal. Unfortunately, the mandate which created the information sharing service was unfunded and the project appears to have languished. A recent visit to the LERPNet portal on LEO revealed the information contained was sparse and dated.

Perhaps to fill this void, several regional law enforcement/retail partnerships have emerged. These regional ORT resources provide a forum where members can report significant issues in their local areas via email bulletins which contain detailed accounts of ORT related issues including suspect and vehicle descriptions, surveillance images, types and value of stolen goods, and investigator point of contact information. The detailed nature of the bulletins allows retail investigators and law enforcement to share information about events and methods of operations used by ORT groups operating in the area. These groups also offer periodic training and/or conferences in ORT related topics.

Albuquerque Retail Assets Protection Association (ARAPA)

Los Angeles Area Organized Retail Crime Association (LAAORCA)

Bay Area Organized Retail Crime Association (BAORCA)

San Diego Organized Retail Crime Association (SDORCA)

Cook County Regional Organized Crime Task Force (CCROC)

Florida Organized Retail Crime Enforcement Network (FORCE)

Metropolitan Area Law Enforcement/Loss Prevention Retail Crimes Networking Group (Pennsylvania, Maryland, D.C., Virginia)

Washington State Organized Retail Crime Association (WSORCA)

Utah Organized Retail Crime Association (UORCA)

Colorado Organized Retail Crime Association (COORCA)

FINCEN

FinCEN is an organization established by the Department of the Treasury that collects, analyzes, and disseminates intelligence on financial crimes. Its mission is to provide a government wide, multisource intelligence and analytical network to support law enforcement agencies in the detection, investigation, and prosecution of financial crimes. FinCEN assists in the investigations of such crimes as money laundering offenses, Bank Secrecy Act violations, and other offenses of a financial nature, e.g., tax and tariff violations; corruption; treason; and bankruptcy, financial institution, and government contract fraud.

FinCEN's financial database has information from reports that are required to be filed under the Bank Secrecy Act, including the Currency Transaction Report, Report of International Transportation of Currency or Monetary Instruments, Currency Transaction Report by Casinos, and Reports of Foreign Bank and Financial Accounts. Furthermore, FinCEN has access to data from Internal Revenue Service Form 8300 (Reports of Cash Payments Over $10,000 Received in a Trade or Business).

Reports from FINCEN can be used either proactively to investigate suspicious businesses or reactively to research the financial transactions of ORT groups and fencing operations. Some indictors which should heighten an investigators suspicion when proactively reviewing FINCEN information include:

Business checks written to individuals as opposed to legitimate suppliers.

Business checks cashed at the banks from which the checks originated instead of being deposited into another business' bank account.

Business checks written to cash on a regular basis in amounts that exceed a business' petty cash requirement.

Multiple business checks connected to a wholesale merchandise operation written on the same day in amounts less than $10,000.

Multiple money orders in increments of $500 or less deposited into bank accounts where the remitter of the money order is the same as the authorized signers on the bank accounts for which the checks are being deposited.

Subjects of suspicious financial transactions connected to a wholesale merchandise operation all maintaining the same address.

Occupations listed for the subjects of suspicious financial activities that are not commensurate to the volume and type of the financial activities.

Checks negotiated in foreign countries related to suspicious financial transactions.

Cash deposits related to financial activities involving currency in $100 denominations.

FinCEN can be contacted at (800) 767-2825. www.fincen.gov

LEADSONLINE

LeadsOnline is the nation's largest online investigation system for law enforcement, providing rapid electronic access to transactions from thousands of reporting businesses including scrap metal processors, secondhand stores, Internet drop-off stores, and pawn shops across the country, as well as critical information from eBay listings for criminal investigations. LeadsOnline is a helpful tool for identifying potential suspects who dispose of merchandise via one of the participating businesses. LeadsOnline is particularly powerful because it collects information from all 50 states and is able to identify suspects from one particular region or jurisdiction who are disposing of property in another. The service has also partnered with eBay to offer the eBay First Responder service. eBay First Responder is available 24 hours a day, 365 days a year and makes it possible for law enforcement to locate possible stolen merchandise listed for sale or sold on eBay. Information available from eBay First Responder includes:

Seller ID information

Seller listings and sales history

Locate possible stolen merchandise listed for sale or already sold

Provide evidence to assist in prosecution of those responsible for property theft

LeadsOnline provides several other fee based services for law enforcement. However, eBay First Responder is available to law enforcement agencies who do not subscribe to LeadsOnline's other services. The information available from eBay First Responder is the same information available to law enforcement investigators from eBay itself but the LeadsOnline system is faster.

Made in the USA
Middletown, DE
15 March 2016